UPDATED

C000261107

Contents

Liston Knife

"A special tool invented for surgery by Scottish surgeon Robert Liston at a time before anaesthetics when speed made the difference between life and painful death"

Liston Jab

A shot perfected by world champion Sonny Liston. Used to win 50 fights with 39 KOs at a time when opponents knew it brought on severe pain and quite often - swift anaesthesia

His jab was the foundation of Sonny's boxing.

Once he got it going opponents were usually in trouble. He cut off the ring and hypnotised fighters as they desperately sought to combat this weapon with an 84 inch range.

Sonny used the jab to control the fight and control where his opponent was fighting from. He kept opponents at a distance where he could do the damage – but they were struggling to land.

Middle distance was best, not too close, he needed space to get his full power into a punch. Sonny didn't throw too many arm shots, he planted his feet and transmitted his body power through the punch. If opponents tried to get too close Sonny flicked out the jab. Sometimes he left it out for a split second to stop his opponent's momentum and put him off balance. Halfway through a round fighters would get frustrated as they tried to work out how they were going to get past a shot that was always in their face, hitting and hurting.

The second fight with Patterson was a classic

example of Sonny's control. He extended a stiff right arm to hold Floyd off then landed savage left hooks to the body.

Very often fighters moved left to miss the jab but that just brought them closer to Sonny's right. A favourite manoeuvre was to hook off the jab and force fighters to adjust their next shot. The result was frustration again. They might get reckless, start throwing wildly – and Sonny was waiting. He'd slip the shot, step inside and bang! They're in the target area for his right hand and 39 KOs tell the tale of what happens next.

Fighting behind the jab, a longer, stronger jab than anything else out there – Sonny didn't get reckless. At his best he didn't need to.

When he had to defend he was the big target – who was hard to score against. The head was constantly moving, side to side, the elbows close in, the right hand high. When a punch did land – his chin was hard. Overlaid across everything was an unnatural strength that partly came from training but mostly from deep inside. Somewhere in Sonny's ancestry there was a line of big, powerful men and they'd passed the body strength on.

Add the flexibility of a top athlete, the stamina to skip rope for nine minutes, plus reflexes so sharp he could snatch a bird out of the air.

Now you're beginning to get an idea of how formidable the man was.

Introduction
Sonny - and other sinners

Charles Sonny Liston was always accused of being associated with the Mob, the Mafia, the underworld. It's certainly true that convicted mobsters like Frank Carbo and Blinky Palermo were pulling strings and taking lumps out of his winnings.

But that wasn't unusual in the fight game where fighters were victims as well as heroes. World champion Joe Louis, who served the sport and his country so well, was exploited by his management throughout his career - and died broke. In his last days Sonny, who admired Joe, was talking to Vegas mobsters about another fight – despite warnings from the Brown Bomber.

Outside the ropes boxing was glamorous as well as lucrative and with the earnings went power. The fight game attracted men like the notorious lawyer Roy Cohn who assisted Senator Joe McCarthy in the Red Scare hearings of the fifties. He was part of an organisation that promoted the Liston/Patterson championship fights.

Cohn had a string of clients including Carlo Gambino, head of the Gambino crime family, 'Fat Tony' Salerno, boss of the Genovese Mob and the 'Teflon Don' himself, John Gotti.

Also on the client list was a rising young New York businessman. Over the dozen years of their association Cohn claimed to have taught him many important lessons including, 'Attack opponents, never admit you're wrong and always claim victory in the press.' According to Cohn lies and smears weren't wrong, they were key strategies. He told him "Never apologize" and 'All publicity is good publicity.'

Many say the businessman, Donald J. Trump, is still following his advice.

Cohn and Trump got together when the Justice Department accused the Trump family of racial discrimination in renting their apartments. In keeping with his 'Attack' strategy Cohn launched a 100 million dollar counter suit. He also accused the Department of using Nazi Gestapo tactics, even though the prosecutor was Jewish. The battle was long and bitter but on this occasion Cohn lost. Trump was forced to place advertisements saying Black tenants were welcome. Cohn made sure the settlement included a statement that Trump "Did not admit to any wrongdoing."

By the end of his career of his career Sonny had earned enough to escape the harassment of landlords. His Vegas mansion was in a high profile neighbourhood next to a golf course. Extras included a pool and a tree house, his car was the latest Fleetwood Cadillac.

Sonny rose from a swamp of deprivation and earned his money the hard way, in the ring. Strength, intimidation and sheer physical presence served him well. One opponent said his jab "made you hurt all over." Press reports described how his right hand arrived like a "small train crash."

The 'Big Bad Bear' is easily inside any list of the top ten heavyweights of all time. He deserves to be remembered for a lot more than the two defeats against Ali *and they can be explained with a lot more honesty than is usually the case.*

This book attempts to do that and add some balance to the full story of Sonny's life and career.

Boxing has a rich history of hard sweat and courage that sometimes looks insane. Equally there are allegations of fight fixing and cheap corruption that cling to the sport.

But if everyone is to be judged only by the company they keep – we need to look a lot further than the sport of boxing. All the way to the world of politics?

So let's have a look at Sonny's many achievements in the ring and try to bring some justice to his legacy.

"When you haven't eaten for 2 days you'll understand"

That's what Jack Dempsey said when he was asked about motivation in boxing. He explained that in his young days he was often knocked down, mainly because he was a teenager fighting grown men. "But to get paid I had to win and if you haven't eaten that's all the motivation you need."

As a teenager Sonny Liston wasn't fighting in bars like Dempsey but he was down and out and hungry. He'd run away from home and beatings handed out by his brutal father, he went looking for his mother. Strangely, considering the problems he was to have with the police for most of his life, he was helped at first by a couple of policemen who found him asleep on a bench in the middle of the night. When he told them there was nothing to eat at home they took him to the police station and fed him in exchange for doing jobs like cleaning cars and generally helping out. An arrangement like that was never going to last and Sonny moved on to a series of amateurish robberies that landed him in jail. But in another twist his prison time opened a door. It was the making of him as a future heavyweight champion. He was introduced to boxing because the ring was a feature of prison life. This was a way for some of the excess energy to be worked out in a disciplined way that might also teach some life lessons.

Twenty five years later he'd moved from a cell in Missouri State Penitentiary to the White House and a meeting with Vice President Lyndon B. Johnson. After destroying Floyd Patterson in the ring Sonny was now heavyweight champion. The photo opportunity was both an image builder for Sonny and an attempt to use the title positively. To show that in America it was possible to rise from the poorest of backgrounds, make mistakes and still achieve something great.

Lyndon Johnson was onboard with ideas like that and anyway President Kennedy had publicly supported Patterson. White House rivalries being what they were LBJ was happy enough to distance himself from the Kennedy clan. "He got that wrong, big time!" the Vice President gleefully told an associate.

Sonny always hoped his own story could be inspirational. That wasn't to be, important factions in politics and the police were determined that wasn't going to happen. Headlines focused on the negatives and the police continued to harass him. Sonny didn't help himself, he was aggressive and drank too much but the police didn't need a reason. Underneath it all the problem was race. Sonny wasn't accepted and the reception when he brought the title back home was one of the great disappointments of his career.

FBI chief J. Edgar Hoover was paranoid about him. The raw power he showed when he beat Patterson so easily touched a nerve, brought out his racism and insecurity. He pursued Sonny as fiercely as Martin Luther King and other Civil Rights activists, keeping his own file on him. Hoover was furious about the meeting with LBJ, "I thought Johnson was smarter than that," he muttered to his deputy and close companion Clyde Tolson. "Liston's dangerous, a Mob fighter." Attitudes like that surrounded Sonny and contributed to his surly attitudes when he was constantly questioned by white journalists. "They're stupid," he told a sparring partner. "They ask stupid questions. They look up at the sun and ask if it's shining."

Part of Hoover's frustration with Sonny was that he was never able to prove any Mob connection. He knew for certain that the first fight with Ali wasn't fixed but refused to say so. "Let everyone think the Mafia own him and he threw it," he told Tolson. "Keeps him in his place."

If he was only looking to protect the White House from Mob influence he could have started in the Oval office. At the time President Kennedy was in a relationship with the girlfriend of Chicago Mob boss Sam Giancana. Of course Hoover knew that but it suited him to hold the information as an unused threat, "I've got Kennedy where I want him," he boasted to his inner circle.

Sonny's jail time didn't leave him bitter, didn't affect his psychology, he was a student of hard times. "I never minded prison," he said on one of the rare times a journalist got more than a scowl and a growl out of him. "Three meals a day and somewhere to sleep." Of course the biggest reason for his relaxed attitude was that no prisoner would consider crossing Sonny and warders would think twice. As one said years later, they knew it would take at least three to handle him. "He wasn't normal, he could beat up two big guys at the same time, easy. But he never went looking for trouble. Leave him alone and he'd leave you alone." Usually. There was one time when he jumped in to contemptuously slap a white gang leader across the face when he saw him hassling a prisoner in the yard. "You get that every time you hit a coloured boy. If you don't like it I'll see you later." That was a long speech for Sonny and it worked. They'd all seen him in prison boxing matches.

Sonny didn't always react to racism. If it suited him he'd let it go. But often he'd react, not verbally, that wasn't his style. Usually the menace of his presence, the look, was enough. If not he'd move, quickly. Apart from alcohol, and Sonny often drank too much, race was the trigger for many of his problems with authority. In the racist sixties a powerful and violent black man was an almost compulsive nightmare.

Then there was his success. As Sonny made money he enjoyed showing it. The sight of him in a pink Cadillac with a white girlfriend was too much for places like St Louis and its long history of police shootings. In 2017 the St Louis record of police shootings was double that of cities like New Orleans, Chicago and Philadelphia. If he hadn't left he would have been shot.

Catholic priests attached to the prison decided to see just how much ring potential Sonny had. If he had the makings of a fighter they could put his case to the parole board and get him released to the care of a trainer and manager. They arranged for the top local professional to come in and take him on. Two rounds was enough, "That's it," the shaken pro said. "No more with this guy."

Thanks to the efforts of the priests, a Catholic layman and a former boxer turned trainer, Sonny was released on parole in October 1952. His long, stormy rise to the heights had begun.

Powerhouse Sonny

Sonny wasn't an oversized heavyweight. At just over six feet he was much shorter than modern fighters like 6' 9" Tyson Fury, 6' 7" Deontay Wilder, or 6' 6" Anthony Joshua. The difference was in his reach. At 84" he had a 2" advantage over Klitschko and Joshua, an inch more than Wilder. His reach meant he could lean in without getting tagged and hammer the full weight of those massive shoulders into the punch.

"Nobody ever hit me like Sonny," said Nino Valdes, Cuban heavyweight champion and a top contender in his day. Nino only had one more fight after he tangled with Sonny and refused to consider a re-match. When Rocky Marciano was commentating on TV he said, "I wouldn't want to be in there with him." One of the last men to train Sonny, Johnnie Tocco, recalled a day when his timing was off. "He kept missing the speed bag with his hook, he wasn't getting his weight in so I shifted him around a little. He caught it right and tore it off the chain. Bang! It flew across the gym." Tocco also trained Mike Tyson and George Foreman but said, "Sonny was the hardest puncher of them all." Another trainer, Sandy Saddler, said Sonny hit a sparring partner so hard, "His headgear flew off and we all thought his head was in it!"

There are many stories of Sonny and his strength. When he visited London on a European tour in '63 as world champion he entertained journalists in the Savoy hotel by lifting a massive oak door off its hinges. It was a trick he'd been taught by a circus strongman and the performance amused him just as much his audience.

Another favourite was lifting up a car and once he went further by overturning it – while the driver and passengers were sitting inside. Sonny would have been happiest if it was a police car but instead it belonged to some business rivals of his management who quickly changed their minds about a deal because, "You wouldn't want Sonny to come knocking on your door one night, would you?" When it came to physical *toughness* a police chief gave Sonny a write up, "Four guys couldn't get the cuffs on him and they were hitting him with their sticks all the time. He was someone you wouldn't go near if you were by yourself."

"Nobody's gonna beat Liston 'cept old age,"

Joe Louis

Fighters, trainers, sparring partners all knew what Sonny Liston had. When Muhammad Ali was asked what he considered his greatest boxing achievement he said, "Beating Sonny Liston".

Many of the people who didn't appreciate Sonny were the journalists of the day. Some feared him. When one said maybe the reason he relied on his left so much was because his right wasn't so powerful, Sonny asked him, "Would you like to find out how hard I hit with my right hand?" One of his trainers, Al Braverman, tried to convince them that

Sonny was a fun guy who liked to play tricks, "He has a water pistol, he's always fooling around." None of the journalists could picture that scene but George Foreman who worked with him as a young sparring partner knew him in a way they didn't. "I loved Sonny. He was a good guy underneath. I admired the way he tried to take on the world and I tried to take on a few of those characteristics. Kids loved him, they thought he was a wonderful guy, they seemed to gravitate towards him."

That sort of picture never reached the press, he was always the bad guy and most of the reporters rejoiced at his downfall against Ali.

But concentrating on those two controversial defeats gives a twisted picture. There was always more to Sonny than that. He came from south of nowhere to be champion of the world.

Competition at the time was savage, boxing was one of the few roads out of the ghetto. The fight game was big news, a major sport with a growing following across society, rich and poor. Typically that brought race and social problems.

The fifties where Sonny began weren't that far from the era of the fearsome black champion Jack Johnson. There was a desperate search to find a 'Great White Hope' to beat Johnson. Jim Jeffries was brought out of retirement to 'wipe that golden smile off his face' as the writer Jack London put it. Because apart from beating up white men in the ring, Johnson was rich and successful. That hurt.

He wasn't shy about showing his wealth either. A newspaper report said Johnson, "Partied, whored, seduced white women, ran night clubs, drove fancy cars." Then on top of that he beat the over-the-hill Jeffries to a pulp in the desert heat of Reno, Nevada. He clearly enjoyed doing it. In the ring he taunted his opponent, asking, "Is that the best you got Mr Jeffries?" After his win there were riots all over the country. The white supremacists of the day came out to whip up hatred and 20 African Americans were lynched. In his biography the straight talking Johnson laid it all out, "It wasn't just about the championship, it was my own honor, the honor of my race, the white hope had failed."

Sonny wasn't as outspoken about race as Jack Johnson but he knew which way the dice were loaded. Asked about white opponents he said "I try to knock them out, it's the best chance I got." Another version of the conversation has Sonny saying "I try to kill them." He had various replies depending on his mood. Asked how he felt about an opponent before a fight he said "I'd like to run him over with a truck." After the NAACP committee said they didn't want Floyd Patterson to defend his title against him Sonny commented, "I'd leave tyre marks."

The fight game wasn't so commercially developed when Johnson was fighting but he helped to build it. He was the world champion and he had the personality to pull in the crowds, even if most of them wanted to see him get hammered. He made money and he called some of the shots. Throughout his life he was determined not to play by the rules of the white establishment.

Sonny had been so poor he was happy to work with white managers and promoters so long as he got paid. He said Blinky Palermo and Frank Carbo, two of the most notorious, were "The best managers I had." They kept him fighting regularly and earning well. Blinky boasted "There was a time in the forties and fifties when we promoted every heavyweight championship fight."

Jake LaMotta admitted he did a deal with them to throw a fight so he could get a crack at the middleweight crown in 1949. Angelo Dundee and his promoter brother Chris left New York to open a gym in Florida so they could get away from Mob influence.

Sonny knew he was exploited but he was doing a lot better than anyone else who came out of his background. In a remark the single-minded Jack Johnson would never have made, Sonny told a lawyer, "If I get the electric chair make sure George Katz (his manager at the time) gets 10% of the juice."

There's no doubt Sonny had an intimidating presence. It began with his size, he didn't need to raise his voice. People he didn't know were given 'The look'. The 'Stoneface' tag wasn't an invention, it was just there. Sonny looked like a champion, dressed like one in a sharkskin suit cut to make his massive shoulders look ever bigger. He had a feeling for how a fighter should present himself. Talking about music he said, "One day somebody's gonna write a blues for fighters. It'll just be for slow guitar, soft trumpet and a bell." Boxing always prospers when there are fighters with a special edge. Menace is a big part of a fighter's weaponry and Sonny had plenty.

Would the Klitschko brothers have reigned so long if he'd been around? Almost certainly not.

Sonny would fight anybody and everybody. But plenty didn't want to fight him. After he retired as the only undefeated heavyweight champion ever, Rocky Marciano was asked what he thought about Liston. "I wouldn't fancy that left hand" was the instant reply. Jim Wicks, manager of British champion Henry Cooper said "We don't even want to meet him walking down the street."

"I wouldn't bet on a grizzly bear against Liston"

Teddy Bentham, fight trainer

As he sat on his stool after taking a first round hammering from Cleveland Williams, Sonny thought he could survive – and win.

He was in his prime in April 1959 when he fought Williams for the first time. Nobody knew his age for certain, he could have been 27 or 32. But he was in rugged condition, training hard and listening to his trainers, something he didn't always do later.

Williams was a big test because although Sonny was a top ten heavyweight, his career could still go either way. Would he get the right fights or would he blocked out by fighters who were more acceptable? At this stage nobody knew.

Outside the ring Sonny was in trouble all the time. Sometimes it looked as if he was deliberately looking for confrontation with the police. At other times they arrested him for no reason, they just wanted to needle him.

But he was beginning to swing his wrecking ball against the class heavyweights of his day. Before he fought Liston, Williams had 47 fights and only lost three. He won 32 by KO and was on an eleven fight streak. Williams could punch with both hands and most of his fights ended early. He was taller than Sonny with an even longer reach. This was a top drawer fighter, rated 22 in the list of all time heavyweights when he was inducted into the Hall of Fame.

Williams was known as the Big Cat because of his almost sleepy style. But there was nothing laid back about his punching. From the bell he tore into Liston and the formidable Sonny was rocked.

Yet the street wise fighter went back to his corner with a glint in his eye. He knew that if he had any weakness, in his chin, his body or his heart, he would have been found out. That never happened. He said later that he knew Williams had to keep that first round barrage up for another nine rounds to beat him. Sonny didn't think he could do that, especially if he got hit with a few of his bombs along the way. He set out to stalk the big cat.

He was patient, knowing that his left jab had started the demolition job. Piece by piece the Big Cat was falling apart. Cleveland was hurting and a left hook that came out of a cluster of punches put him down in the third. He got up, not knowing what was happening and went down again. The referee stopped it and Williams didn't bother to argue. When they fought again Sonny was even more confident. He told his manager at the time, Pep Barone, he had Cleveland all worked out.

Next stop was Chicago and Nino Valdes, a fighter good enough to have troubled Rocky Marciano's shrewd management team so much he never got to fight the champion. Once again Sonny won a third round stoppage. He hit Valdes with a left hook that sent him staggering, then caught him with a combination. A final right hand smash knocked him out in 47 seconds of the third. It was his 18th win in a row and Sonny was buzzing.

Number nineteen was Willi Besmanoff a tough fighter who had never been knocked off his feet. Sonny stopped him on a cut eye at the end of the sixth. He complained afterwards that he wasn't at his best and started too slowly. What's more likely is Sonny was told not to end the fight too soon. He was popular on television and fans wanted to see more of him.

Besmanoff wasn't just another notch on Sonny's gun. There was something significant about the fight. In Besmanoff's corner was a certain Angelo Dundee who got an early close up of Sonny's work.

Ever the observer and professor, Angelo filed away a few notes he would use in the future. "I saw how dangerous Sonny was, the way he used his reach and jab. But by the end Sonny was starting to blow and I thought maybe his stamina won't hold up too well against someone who moves like Ali." By the time he came to work Ali's corner in a title fight, Angelo had a plan.

Man From Cut N Shoot Knocked Down And Out

Roy Harris was from a small town in Texas called Cut N Shoot and definitely the biggest story to come out of there. Cus D'Amato, manager of Floyd Patterson, called him the second best heavyweight in the world at one time but that was most likely a pitch to boost Floyd, who beat Harris in a title fight.

In a five year career Harris was undefeated until he met Patterson but he never fought men like Eddie Machen or Zora Folley who would have spoiled that record.

Harris believed he had a real chance of beating Patterson in a re-match. Fighting Liston was a misguided effort to get back at Patterson – a big mistake because Sonny was on a roll. It was only just over a month since he had taken out Cleveland Williams in their second fight, knocking him out in the second round.

Sonny had a sixteen pounds weight advantage and a huge edge in confidence coming into the ring. He said before the fight that if Harris was still standing after 10 rounds they should give him it. Sonny didn't plan on going half that distance.

As usual he was moving in behind the left jab and Harris was trying to work out why it was so easy for Liston to tag him. Even when he thought he was safe and out of distance - Sonny's long reach found him. He was moving well. Fast and fresh, head moving tick tock from side to side, never giving Harris an easy shot.

Halfway through the first round Sonny landed a monster left hook that put Harris down and virtually ended the fight. The Texan fighter was game, he got up four times before the referee stopped it. Harris went on to have a good career though he was never in Sonny's league. Who was?

Some time after the fight Sonny told a story to the writer Mark Kram that was quoted by Nick Tosches in his great book about Sonny, 'The Devil And Sonny Liston'. Sonny said that after the fight he was alone and dozing in a chair in the lobby of the hotel where he was staying. He heard footsteps behind him and a gun clicked as the barrel was put behind his ear.

A man said, "Don't look round – Nigger." He told Sonny there was one bullet in the chamber and it had his name on it – unless he said, "I'm a no good, yeller Nigger."

Whoever it was sounded upset that Sonny had made Roy Harris, a white fighter, 'look a fool tonight' and Sonny was a 'Bad Nigger.' Sonny agreed to do what he said and the man walked away after telling him not to look round. In his book Nick Tosches wonders if Sonny made the story up. Maybe it didn't happen exactly like that but bearing in mind what happened to Sonny over the years it's believable. Joe Louis once described how shocked he was to discover that his trainer Jack Blackburn, who was black, was carrying a gun at one of his fights. When he asked why Blackburn said, "We're in the South."

Kram said Sonny told him "People are violent" and it was "torture" to be in public places. Who knows whether the story was true? But Sonny was certainly around violent people, white and black, for most of his fight career.

Sonny's next fight was against Zora Folley who was in the top ten ratings, together with Sonny. Cus D'Amato had decided he was another fighter to be kept away from Floyd Patterson for as long as possible. He succeeded, Zora never did get to fight Floyd and the dangerous Cleveland Williams never did either.

But Folley was always ready for a fight and three months after he decked Roy Harris, Sonny was ducking through the ropes in Denver, ready to take him on.

Folley was a Korean War veteran who won five stars in battle. There was no chance he would be intimidated as other fighters were. Folley won the first round easily; at one point he hit Sonny with seven right hands and a couple of combinations without a serious reply.

Whether Sonny decided to carry the fight to Folley, or his corner told him to step up, we'll never know. But from the bell in the second he got the left jab to work, waiting for the opening he knew would come. Then he hit Folley with a right that put him down like a fallen tree.

Folley got up at nine and made his way to the centre of the ring where Sonny was waiting, in no particular hurry. He knew what was going to happen next. He blocked a couple of punches with his massive forearms then let go with another right and down went Folley – but again he got up at nine. This time the bell saved him temporarily. He lasted just seconds into the third before another right hand switched his senses off and this time he didn't get up.

Afterwards he said, "Just think, I was told, don't worry about his right."

It was Sonny's twenty first knockout in thirty one fights. Folley said he thought Patterson would be too quick for Sonny. If Sonny heard that he would have smiled. He knew Patterson's handlers didn't think the same.

Sonny's next fight against Eddie Machen went 12 rounds mainly because Machen was determined to grab and hold and refused to make a fight of it. Sonny won the decision by a mile but if Floyd Patterson watched it he should have learned something. Sonny could be frustrated and stopped from landing his bombs. Sonny's comment later was, "It takes two to dance and Machen wasn't in the mood."

But the truth was Sonny could not get to Machen. He was frustrated, and as he chased his man the lunging attacks missed their target. The all conquering Sonny didn't look so impressive. It was a glimpse of what was to come in his first fight with Ali.

Once again Sonny was being watched and studied. Angelo Dundee's file was growing.

Meanwhile Cus D'Amato was still determined to keep Sonny away from Floyd Patterson. The more he saw of Sonny the less he liked the idea of them in the ring together. At one point Sonny went to D'Amato's office unannounced and asked if he was going to get a shot. He was the obvious contender. But Cus had been in the fight game a long time, he knew he could stall Sonny for a while.

Sonny's handlers wanted to keep the pressure up, they knew so long as he kept on winning they would get a shot at the title. A couple of warm-ups were arranged so Sonny would stay on the edge, primed and ready to explode.

The next fight was in Miami Beach against Howard King, a solid journeyman fighter Sonny had stopped in eight rounds the year before. Sonny was expected to win but King would give him a workout and a fight night was better than more gym time and training that sometimes frustrated him.

Sonny took the first round, coming out aggressively behind the left lead and trying to land his right cross. His best shot was a right to the body that reminded King, painfully, of the last time they fought.

King started the second round better, trying to back him up, using speed to upset his rhythm. Sonny quickly adjusted and landed a cluster of punches, putting King down for a count of nine.

He made it to the end of the round but after 46 seconds of the third round it was all over when Sonny drove in a left to the body and followed up with a thundering right that put King down and out.

It was the thirty third win and twentieth knock out in a career that was getting better by the month. In the three years before he fought Patterson for the title Sonny had eleven fights. The fight game was more box office oriented then, with packed stadiums and busy fighters. A contrast to the Klitschko era when the brothers would fight around once a year.

Apart from Machen, Sonny won all those fights on a KO. The last one before Patterson was the most spectacular of them all. Worryingly for Cus D'Amato, it actually happened on the undercard of a Patterson title defence.

Some observers said it looked as if Liston hit Albert Westphal with a club, such was the power of the right hand he landed in round one. Westphal was heavyweight champion of Germany and rated number four in the world but on the evidence of this fight he probably should not have been in the same ring as Sonny.

The ringside commentator said Westphal had respect for Sonny and his left jab. The respect took the form of back pedalling at speed, counter clockwise, trying to miss it. But other fighters had tried that and Sonny was especially sharp that night. At the weigh-in Westphal asked Sonny why he was so angry with him. Sonny told him to wait until the night.

Early on he caught Westphal with a couple of jabs that speeded up his retreat and it was just a matter of time. Sonny landed another jab then a short right that pitched Westphal straight down, face forward. The count was unnecessary; he never moved and was unconscious for another two minutes. Asked if he ever wanted to fight Sonny again he said no, he'd never been hit so hard and would not be coming back for more.

Afterward Sonny referred to him as 'quick fall '. Probably no disrespect intended but he hurried back to his dressing room to watch the Patterson fight. Concentrating closely and saying nothing he saw the champion win then made a single comment. "He's missing a lot of punches." That was enough for Sonny. He knew he would dominate against Patterson from the off.

But he was getting very angry with the title fight situation – though that problem was about a lot more than boxing.

"There's good guys and bad guys"

Sonny Liston to the press before he fought Patterson

At the beginning of the sixties Sonny Liston and the Kennedy brothers were at the peak of their powers. Travelling from opposite ends of society they had arrived together in the spotlight. According to some Sonny was the most dangerous man on the planet.

According to others he was the baddest. JFK and his brother Bobby were confronted by the Cuban missile crisis, Civil Rights riots and a confident Mafia that some said was second only to the National Government in power.

On the surface Sonny and the Kennedy brothers were poles apart. Liston was born into poverty, put to work as a child and brutalized by an uncaring father. Trying to survive on the streets he inevitably got into trouble. His education was in prison, the Kennedy clan had everything money could buy and then some.

Their father was immensely rich. He invested while many of his contemporaries were going broke in the thirties. Stock market rules were lax and he profited from what would be called 'insider' trading today. He made millions out of Hollywood studios, the oil business and real estate. Joseph P. Kennedy was the 15th richest man in America and a father with ambitions for his sons. He would have liked to be a mover and shaker on the political stage himself but realised he had too many bodies buried in his overflowing cupboards. He may have involved with the bootleggers of alcohol prohibition days.

The Mob has always been keen to cultivate legitimate businessmen to gain an inside track and Joe's connections extended to the top layers of the Mafia. It has been speculated that Joe called in favours to help his son Jack win the tight points decision over Nixon in the 1960 presidential election. Naturally the Mob does not do favours for free. They were expecting the Kennedy administration to cut them some slack. When that didn't happen and Attorney General Robert Kennedy started a personal

crusade against them, and corrupt union leader Jimmy Hoffa in particular, the atmosphere started to crackle with violence. This was a familiar story, a Hollywood story.

Even looking at it from the other end of the telescope, Sonny couldn't fail to see the connections between power, big money and the Mob.

From where he was standing their ways were appealing. Getting the right fights wasn't easy. Without connections in the fifties you'd be fighting in the small towns, in small arenas for peanuts.

In so many areas of American life, from show biz to boxing to politics the Mob was there, protecting their interests and looking for a share of the action. Their influence was useful to any businessman looking to cut corners.

Down the line, when the Kennedys came to power - Sonny was caught up in the politics. There was only one world heavyweight boxing title, in those days. The crown carried genuine international prestige. So the softly spoken, well mannered Floyd Patterson was a good champion. The FBI had finally removed men like Carbo from the scene and it was time to start a new era.

Patterson's clean image worked alongside the Civil Rights movement. Sonny's menace and his management sent out the wrong signals. In Kennedy's case, particularly the patriarch Joe, you could say it was too close to home.

JFK's own links to the Mob were unknown at that time. By modern tabloid standards the press was invisible. The Kennedy sex drive was roaring along, he said he got a headache if he didn't have sex with somebody new every day. His womanising was never mentioned in any news outlet. Think for a moment about today's social media then think about the top Hollywood star of the day, Marilyn Monroe, being in the headlines – and in bed – with the President. Not a word was said.

But Sonny Liston as heavyweight champion? No, not appropriate. Hypocrisy was a way of life and would continue to be. Sonny knew the score. It wasn't just Cus D'Amato who was keeping him out of the ring with Patterson. In one of his rare comments to the press he said, 'There are good guys and bad guys. But one day soon, the bad guy is gonna win."

What eventually worked for him in getting a fight for the championship was Floyd Patterson's decency and pride. It was obvious Liston was the top contender, he had been dodged for a long time and Cus D'Amato wanted to keep it that way. He was dreaming up fresh excuses every week. Cus knew Floyd couldn't survive in the same ring as Sonny.

The manager's first line of defence was that the champion wasn't going to get involved with someone who had Mob connections. He spoke out against their control of the sport. But others say D'Amato wasn't so clean himself and what he really wanted was to swap mob control – for control by himself and the heavyweight title was key.

But journalists were increasingly asking, 'Is Floyd afraid of Liston, why is he not giving him a shot?'

Floyd was often described as a gentleman, particularly when journalists wanted to contrast him with Sonny. But finally he did the right thing and insisted Sonny got his title shot. The fight was originally scheduled for New York but the New York commission refused to sanction it because of Liston's prison time so it was moved to Chicago.

Fans paid $4 million at the Comiskey stadium and the fight was shown in 260 theatres. All they got was two minutes and five seconds of the first round. The reason? Floyd Patterson had a disastrous rush of blood to the head.

He'd been told to start slow and fight out of the defensive, low crouch D'Amato had taught him. He would also box Peek-A-Boo style with both hands high, protecting his chin. D'Amato's thinking was that if Patterson could get through the early rounds he might just snatch a points win as Sonny tired later on. Nothing wrong with the strategy, Patterson was the problem. From the bell, probably stung by all the taunts about him being scared of Liston, he abandoned defence and rushed forward – taking the fight to the challenger.

Rarely has a bigger mistake been made. Patterson was lunging at Liston, leaving gaps for the left jab that wasn't just a jab. It was more like the ram used in medieval times to batter down the castle gates. It only needed one to wobble Patterson and as he suddenly remembered all D'Amato's warnings - it was too late.

Floyd was trapped on the ropes as Sonny hammered him with jabs. A final thunder blow to the cheek put Patterson down and out. Afterwards he couldn't remember what happened, his brain was wiped clean.

Some claimed he went down too easily but nobody could stand up to Sonny's close range jabs. The doubters probably didn't see the punches that did the damage. Liston wasn't a flashy puncher, anyone not following the action closely would miss the mini earthquakes that landed.

Sonny's win wasn't well received at the White House. The brothers probably thought it was just another Mafia fix with more money to be made when there was a return. They understood that brand of deal but this time they were wrong.

Although Sonny never met the Kennedys their careers did have some crossovers. Sonny's former undercover manager Frankie Carbo was an early target for Attorney General Robert Kennedy. Carbo was taken out of the boxing scene – at least 25 years too late – and given a 25 year prison sentence.

Cus D'Amato promised the return fight would see a different Patterson, more disciplined, with more movement. At least he would be prepared because now he had the experience of meeting Sonny in the ring. Was that a good thing? The Patterson camp thought so. Deep down he worried.

The new champion was 21 lbs heavier, making Floyd look the light heavyweight he truly was. Sonny was booed in the introductions, Patterson thinly cheered. Ali made a cameo appearance in the ring and pretended to be scared of Sonny. Many a true feeling . . . is often expressed as a joke.

The referee calls the fighters together and as they face each other Sonny looks comfortably bigger, Floyd looks down at the floor.

Inside the first minute Sonny has landed the jab and a right hand. When he is attacked early in a fight he makes himself a harder target, the head is moving constantly as he moves forward on the counter. Not so Patterson. He crouches down but as he comes up he runs straight into an uppercut that sends him sprawling. He gets up too soon and tries to hang on but he can't hold the champion in a clinch. Sonny's body power pulls him free and now he has Patterson where he wants him. His right is planted on Patterson's shoulder, holding him there as he works away at the body with his left. Every shot counts until the referee pulls them apart - and exposes Patterson to more devastation. A two handed attack sends him stumbling round the ring until he goes down.

As he takes the standing count he looks bewildered, what is he doing here? One thing he does know, he must go again. Pride and courage drive him on. But he's never felt more like an ex-champion. Liston is a force he can't handle.

The brutal truth is he can't defend himself and the fight should be stopped. But this is the world heavyweight title. Hoping desperately that he can – somehow - make it to the bell Patterson throws a right hand then ducks away. Liston slips it, moves to his right and now Patterson is opened up. Two right hands to the side of his head and a whipping left uppercut finish him.

"You're blowin' it son, you're blowin' it" *The kind of advice Sonny needed in his corner.*

Nothing about Sonny Liston's career was ever simple and uncomplicated but one thing can be said. Put Angelo Dundee in his corner and not Ali's, and you might just have changed boxing's history books.

Some experts say that Angelo was a good trainer, not a great one. But as a corner man he was in a class of his own. Ali might never have got in the ring with Sonny – if Angelo hadn't saved him in the Henry Cooper fight. Ali got too clever for his own good and Henry caught him with a left hook that put him down.

Luckily for the Ali camp it was near the end of the round. When Angelo got him back to the corner he made a small split in his boxer's glove bigger, then called over the referee. The official immediately called for a new glove and the extra time gave Ali the moments he needed to clear his head. He went on to win and keep his place as a contender for Sonny's title.

But one of the greatest corner intervention Angelo made was in the Sugar Ray Leonard Tommy Hearns title fight in 1981. Hearns had fought his way back after Leonard won the early rounds. When Leonard came back at the end of the twelfth round Angelo launched into a rant. He said to Leonard, 'What you doing, you nuts? You're slowing down, fighting his fight. Move, speed, pick it up, not slow like this guy.'

Then came the words the camera caught. As the bell rang for the thirteenth round Angelo's last words to his fighter were, 'You're blowin' it son, you're blowin' it'.

Leonard came off his stool revitalised and tore into the tiring Hearns, driving him round the ring. He nearly won it in that round but in the next the referee stopped it after a tornado of punches had Hearns hanging through the ropes.

The phrase is now part of boxing folk lore. It was motivation based on an exact reading of the fight - and a feeling for what would get his fighter going. Exactly what Sonny needed in his fights with Ali.

But that expertise was in the other corner as Dundee worked on his man, feeding him the knowledge.

Ali's preparation for the Liston fights had started years earlier, long before Ali knew it. Angelo had studied Sonny, waiting for the day when he might be in the other corner. He saw the big bad bear looked less convincing against taller fighters. So he told Ali to stand tall and let Liston know he was the smaller man.

Of course Angelo had seen the battering power of the left jab, the intimidator that made strong men back off. So he told Ali to use his speed and go to the left, away from the jab. 'The way I saw it Ali could neutralize the jab and without it Liston wasn't the same fighter."

But the real pain for Sonny was self inflicted. Sonny just didn't rate Ali as a fighter – or a man. Ali didn't have anything like the same background as Sonny. He'd never had to mix with criminals in prison or struggle on the streets, Ali enjoyed a happy, middle class childhood. In his autobiography he admitted he was afraid of Liston. For his part Sonny thought the younger man was a mouthy kid who would fold when he got to him.

But that was the point, when he got to him. Angelo Dundee knew Ali was even quicker than most people thought, certainly Sonny. To catch Ali he needed to be at the peak of condition but he didn't train as hard as he should have.

Dundee would have made sure he did. The Liston camp made a great point of showing how tough he was by throwing a huge medicine ball at short range right into his stomach. Sonny never flinched but Angelo scoffed saying, 'Why don't they throw it at his head because that's where my guy is going to be hitting him'.

Sonny needed Dundee in his corner when he was struggling and failing to land his jab. He lacked a voice in his ear. Angelo had the stature to tell Sonny what was happening. To yell at him, "Pick it up, get in close, you're fighting his fight". Most of all, to say

"You're blowin' it man, you're blowin' it". Instead Angelo was in the other corner, driving Ali on even after a solution from Liston's gloves got into his eyes. Ali couldn't see and wanted to quit but Angelo wouldn't let him. He sent him out, told him to stick to the ropes and run, stay away till his eyes cleared.

The contrast is there, Sonny did quit on his stool.

But why? Was it because for the first time in his boxing life Sonny couldn't find a way forward? He was frustrated and his jab wasn't working. As Dundee rightly said, without the jab he wasn't so confident. He didn't feel right. Whatever the reason, Sonny quit. He said he had a shoulder injury and couldn't fight on.

"The dumbest thing Sonny ever did"
Geraldine Liston, Sonny's wife

Amongst the thousands of words written about Sonny you won't find any about Sonny the handyman. Although friends agreed he was at his best with children and they loved being with him, he doesn't seem the type to be doing jobs around the house. But before he was a pro fighter and when he was first released from prison one of his managers found him a job labouring in the building industry. It's easy to imagine that with his strength and agility Sonny was handy, an asset on any site.

When he began to make it in the ring boxing was a full time job, fighters kept busy and in training. Sonny would be in demand as a sparring partner - though as he developed not too many fighters would pay to go a few rounds with Sonny!

Especially since he'd definitely take it seriously and could easily damage a hot prospect.

Yet he did have a settled domestic life. By all accounts he and Geraldine were happy together and any time she was interviewed after his death she said, "Sonny was a good husband to me and a good father to the children. He provided for us, he was a kind and gentle man." There are stories of how Sonny would help friends and neighbours who called on him. One woman whose husband fell ill said Sonny could be relied on to come at any time, day or night, to help her lift him if she was in difficulties.

Geraldine was protective of his memory and during his career she was always around to support him. She also told a story which may be the truest explanation of why Sonny quit on his stool in the first Ali fight.

While he was in training for it a friend asked him if he could help him to fix his roof which had been damaged in a storm. Sonny said yes but as they worked on it – he fell off and landed on his shoulder. The fight wasn't very far away and at that stage nobody, including Jack Nilon his manger and Sonny himself, wanted to call it off. They thought he could get through it and that was where they miscalculated.

The problem was Sonny did not take Ali,

Cassius Clay as he was then, seriously enough.

Neither did Jack Nilon. They knew Sonny had a problem but figured Ali wouldn't stick around long enough to worry Sonny. A KO in the early rounds was the likeliest result they thought.

They weren't alone. Ali was untested against class opponents and Sonny's destruction of Patterson over two fights had created an aura of invincibility around him. "He'll hammer that loudmouth kid and a good thing too. Shut him up for good." That was the almost unanimous view around the fight world.

So they took the chance and went ahead. But after the first round Sonny told his corner his left shoulder had gone, the power of his murderous jab wasn't there. He should have pulled out of the fight and treated the shoulder.

Geraldine knew the fall off the roof had damaged him and looking back she bitterly regretted that he went ahead. Sonny's career and their life together could have been completely different she said. It was, "The dumbest thing Sonny ever did and it cost us plenty," she said. "He was sure he could beat Clay, Sonny hated the way he carried on."

The story has the ring of truth and Sonny didn't spar for three days after the fall. His purse was suspended after the fight but eventually there was medical confirmation he was injured and he was paid. Typically there were complications when it was revealed that, unknown to Sonny, his management had invested in a company that was interested in promoting a re-match if Clay won.

It meant Sonny had shares in an outfit that wanted him to lose. This was the tangled world of the sixties fight game but who would be sure it's so much different today?

Then there was the betting angle. The odds on a Clay win were seven to one, the way to make money was to make sure Sonny lost.

The odds were that way because over the years Sonny had created an unbeatable vibe with twenty five knock outs. The New York Times was so sure Clay was in for a beating they sent a young journalist to Miami Beach to check the quickest route from the stadium to the hospital, they wanted that story *first*.

So what's the truth, was Sonny genuinely injured or did he dive? Perhaps the best indicator is his snarling anger when he saw how journalists were reporting his defeat. "That was my title, I won it. Do these bums think I'd throw my title away like that?"

Sonny was many things – but he was no actor. He did try acting, even made a commercial with Andy Warhol, and we could all see. He was no actor. That was genuine anger and regret about what happened.

"Is he the bravest guy you ever fought?"

A re-match with Ali hadn't been written into the contract but it was accepted there would be another one. Sonny certainly wanted it although Ali's backers would have liked an easier fight first.

This time Sonny did the hard work in training, the word was he looked better than ever. He even chatted to the press about where he went wrong in the first fight, saying he should never have run after him but he insisted Ali was only an average fighter, not as gutsy as Floyd Patterson.

There was a change in Sonny's management setup that conspiracy fans might find significant. He was given a new manager, Al Braverman, a tough New Yorker and former heavyweight fighter who went unbeaten from 1938 to '41. He was brought in to keep Sonny in line and training hard. Now, if the Mob wanted Sonny to lose again, would they do that? Again, it's an open question.

Sonny was to meet up with Braverman once more, in his last ever fight, against Chuck Wepner. But this time Al was in the other corner, watching as Sonny's jab cut his man's face to pieces. Wepner was known as the Bayonne Bleeder and after the fight he would need 65 stitches. But the tough ex marine would not quit.

At the end of an early round the referee went across to Wepner's corner. He was worried Wepner was cut so badly round the eyes he couldn't see properly. In truth Wepner could not but he was 'rescued' by Braverman. When the referee held up three fingers and asked him how many, Braverman, standing behind his man and hidden from the referee, tapped him three times.

The fight continued until the referee stopped it in the ninth. Even Sonny was uneasy about what was happening, he told his corner he didn't want to hit him anymore. At the press conference after the fight he was asked if Wepner was the bravest man he had ever fought.

"No," Sonny replied. "His manager is".

Braverman kept up his connection with Chuck Wepner and managed him when he fought Ali. This was another mismatch set up by Don King to give Ali a payday and keep him sweet.

Wepner was delighted, he was going to get the biggest purse of his life, $100,000. He bought his wife a pink negligee and told her that after the fight she would be sleeping with the heavyweight champion of the world.

Journalists who had seen Wepner fight were incredulous he was going in with Ali. They wanted to know how his face would hold out but Al Braverman had an answer.

He said he found a new salve he would smear on Wepner's face. It was a miracle product, no chemist had ever been able to break the formula – and it would stop Wepner's face cutting up. That was some claim after what happened in the Liston fight.

"But wouldn't the referee stop the fight because this salve introduced a foreign body to the ring?"

"No way" said Al, "it's made right here in America."

The story sounds too good to be true and probably is but it is the kind of crack Braverman was capable of. His dialogue was the real thing, straight out of Damon Runyon.

Late on in the fight Wepner pushed Ali over and he fell over. A gleeful Wepner turned round and shouted to Braverman, "get the car running we're going to the bank".

Braverman put him right, "You better turn round, he's getting up and he looks mad as hell." Ali was and the referee stopped the fight after one more minute of punishment for Wepner.

In the dressing room Wepner's wife fingered the negligee and asked him, 'Do I go to Ali's room or is he coming to me?"

Sonny was in terrific shape for the second Ali fight and ready to go when disaster struck. Ali suddenly started vomiting after dinner one night. He was taken to hospital and surgeons decided he needed an immediate operation for hernia.

Sonny's career was in dive-bomb mode from thereon. He lost inspiration and motivation for training. Observers said he appeared burned out, tired and disinterested, as if he had peaked and couldn't get there again. Angelo Dundee sneaked into a training session and reported that Sonny looked terrible when he was sparring and clumsy when he was skipping.

Maybe somebody got to him or the previous training really had taken too much out of him. His conditioning was off, his mind wasn't right. There were rumours Black Muslims had threatened to kill him if he won. Ali was one of their links to the African American community.

When the bell went for the first round Sonny was surprised by the way Ali came out so fast and landed two good right hand punches. He tried to land a jab but missed and finished up unprepared for the lightning right that downed him. He never saw it and down he went.

Afterwards Al Braverman heaped blame on referee Joe Walcott who instead of starting the count kept on pulling Ali away to a neutral corner. But the timekeeper did start the count and by the time

Walcott had got round to thinking about it, Sonny was up.

Walcott wiped his gloves and was set to let the fight continue when he was stopped by a shout from ring historian Nat Fleischer, no friend of Sonny's, that the fight was over. He had been counted out.

The fight wasn't worthy of a world heavyweight championship. It was a disaster, a fiasco, but was it a fix?

Light heavyweight champion Jose Torres who was doing a radio commentary said Sonny had been caught by a perfect shot. The respected trainer Teddy Atlas analysed it like this. "When Sonny throws his left jab his peripheral vision for a split second is blinded. He can't see the right Ali is throwing and that's how he got tagged. It's the ones you don't see that do the damage."

When it was over Angelo Dundee went across to Sonny as he sat in his corner. After he spoke to him and got a good look into his eyes Dundee thought it was a genuine hit and said so. The cynical will reply, "He would, wouldn't he?"

Sonny himself said he was caught by a punch he never saw – though he also said Cleveland Williams had hit him harder.

But Sonny was not the same man who fought Williams, took some hard shots and came back.

That had been six years ago. By now Sonny was probably thirty five, he may have been older. He had a bad night and was caught by a younger, faster and inspired boxer who just possibly was, in his own often repeated words . . . the greatest. Or was there another reason? In that turbulent period with Civil Rights marches, riots and the emergence of the Black Muslim movement other forces were taking an interest in the fight world.

In Sonny's camp some were convinced that the Black Muslims did get to Sonny and threaten to kill him. They said he told Geraldine when she asked what happened. "If I win, I'm dead."

There will always be theories pointing this way and that but after the fight there was one certainty – Sonny was now in deep trouble.

In two brutally short fights against Floyd Patterson he had won, then successfully defended the title. But in two more, totally disastrous fights, he lost everything. His title to Ali, his reputation to boxing's witch hunters and his licence to state commissioners.

Sonny loved being a champion. Now he was just another boxer, past his prime and fighting for eating money. Where he fought didn't matter, the purse did.

The money due to him for the second Ali fight was withheld because the authorities said he had thrown the first fight to cash in on the return. They couldn't prove it but the way he lost meant they got away with it.

What exactly did happen to Sonny's money? The boxing establishment wasn't quite so open about that one. From the ex-champ's point of view the news just got worse. He was barred from boxing in practically every state in the US. So together with Geraldine, her daughter and an adopted daughter, Sonny left for Sweden and the opportunity to earn a living in the ring.

The Swedish fighter Ingemar Johansson, a former world heavyweight champion who defeated Floyd Patterson, was now a national hero and a top promoter. He respected Sonny as a fighter and he knew enough about the boxing world to appreciate the handcuffs Sonny had been forced into to get his title shot. He brought Sonny over - and the ex-champ delivered.

His first fight was with the tough German champion Gerhard Zech who had held his title for three years. Sonny demolished him in the 7th. The thunder puncher was back in business.

Next he knocked out Amos Johnson in the third. As an amateur Johnson had beaten Ali, and the great future light heavyweight champion Bob Foster. But he could not live with Sonny who was knocking opponents over as easily as he did in his prime.

Dave Bailey went in 3 minutes, Elmer Rush was knocked out in the 6th. Sonny was enjoying Sweden.

He was not in the vindictive glare of self important boxing writers who never faced any of the challenges Sonny had - inside and outside the ring.

Sweden liked Sonny too and after one fight a woman asked him and Geraldine to adopt her baby.

The mother explained she thought they would know how to look after children. Her offer was accepted and at last Sonny had a son.

But still there was no welcome home for him in the US – except in California. The West Coast took him in where no other state would. Sonny responded and picked up a new trainer, Dick Saddler the former featherweight champion.

In the ring the fearsome puncher was back, piling up the KO's. Bill McMurray went in the 4th and Billy Joiner in the 7th.

His next opponent was Henry Clark, ranked 5th in the world ratings and champion of California. This was judged to be a real test for the second coming of Sonny. Yet when they were introduced from the ring the difference in size and presence was telling. Sonny seemed to dwarf Clark, who wasn't small.

Angelo Dundee was doing ringside commentary as Sonny went about his business. He had other professional reasons to be there.

At this point Ali was out of the fight game because of his refusal to be drafted into the Vietnam war on religious grounds. Dundee was training Jimmy Ellis, a possible future opponent for Sonny and, as usual, he was making mental notes.

He was impressed by Sonny – and worried for Clark's health. "If he carries on this he's going to take one hell of a beating." According to Dundee, Clark was waiting for Sonny to come onto him, then trying to counter and "Sonny will find him all night".

Ever the connoisseur he was almost drooling over the quality of Sonny's jab. "Beautiful, I love watching it".

Clark was 'catching' the jab to the body and head. With his ranking Clark was a serious contender – before this fight. Sonny wasn't even in the rankings but he systematically, painfully, exposed the difference in class. The jab set Clark up time and again for a right. When he went on the attack Sonny slipped the lead and stepped inside. After a few rounds Dundee could do no more than praise Clark's ability to take punch. At this time Sonny was possibly

36, Clark 23. The fight looked like a boy against a man.

Towards the end of the sixth it was nearly all over. Early in the seventh it was. A big right detached Clark's brain from his body and the referee rightly stopped it.

Before the fight Clark had been explaining how he was man of the year for two years running in San Quentin prison. He used to go there to box exhibitions with cons who knew how to fight. Good for him. The big difference of course was Sonny had been to prison for real. While he was in there he fought for real, in and out of the ring and didn't get to go home afterwards.

Sonny's next opponent was the journeyman fighter Sonny Moore who stepped in as a replacement at the last moment. Sonny's management wanted to keep him active and in training but he was never going to be troubled in this fight. He went for a KO in the first round with a left hook but the referee stepped in between them and probably saved Moore. He gave Moore a standing eight count then let them continue, maybe he wanted to give the crowd a long fight. Sonny was lumbering along, slightly overweight but he caught up with Moore in the third landing a vicious left hook to the body that put him down.

One of Sonny's better sides was revealed after the fight. He was guaranteed a purse of $12,500 but took $9,800 so other fighters on the bill could get paid more. It was a nice touch from Sonny, the ex-champ looking after lesser pros.

Nobody knew exactly how old Sonny was at that time but when he was in full training he was still lethal. All referees had to do was count to 10. In just two months in Sweden he had left four fighters stretched out on the canvas. Now he was back in the States he carried right on.

 Boxing is different today but, even if they had the opportunity, not many established fighters would relish a schedule like that.

By now, with Ali deprived of his title, Sonny was a powerhouse in waiting. But Jimmy Ellis and Joe Frazier were the two main contenders. Liston should have been with them but as the wise old pro Archie

Moore said, "He won't get a chance, he's too strong for them."

Archie knew his fight game and he was on the money. Sonny never got another shot and the rest wasn't history. It was tragedy.

"All Of Life Is Six To Five against"

Damon Runyon

Boxing has always attracted great writers like Ernest Hemingway, Budd Schulberg and Norman Mailer. The journalist and author Damon Runyon came from an earlier generation but he was even closer to boxing than they were.

Sonny Liston and Damon Runyon would have recognised each other as fellow spirits. They never met but they operated in the same kind of world.

Runyon took his vocabulary and style from the New York underworld and turned it into a unique form which has never been equalled. His stories were filled with characters like Bookie Bob, Harry the Horse and Dave the Dude. He would have been at home with men like Blinky Palermo and Mr Grey, other wise known as Frankie Carbo. The sort of people who lived dangerously and were to be seen at training camps. Their conversations were his stories.

He gave world light heavyweight champion Slapsie Maxie Rosenbloom his ring name and christened Jim Braddock the Cinderella man. Boxing and the ways of the fight world were his bread and butter.

Throughout his career Sonny was associated with the Mafia. Given his desperate start in life it was simple practicality, Sonny wasn't exactly holding the best hand.

Damon Runyon understood that kind of situation. Writing about boxing and horse racing, as he often did, he said his time at the track had given him a way of looking at the world.

All of life, he decided, is six to five against. But in Sonny's case the odds were longer.

Life had taught him a different lesson. It was one Runyon knew too. If you rub up against the money, some of it may stick to you.

It's entirely possible that Damon Runyon knew Frank Carbo in his younger days before he managed to get such a grip on boxing. Carbo was a genuine boxing fan who got into the game because he could control it, make money – and he enjoyed the fights.

Sonny knew the downsides of the company he was keeping. The priests who played a key role in his early days spelled them out. But who else was going to get him fights, keep him supplied with money and help him out of tricky situations?

In much the same way JFK's father Joe saw business, and sometimes personal advantages, in working with them. Once after he had crossed the wrong person he called on the Mob for protection. His sons saw the advantages too but there was more danger for them. They could hide the links from the public but not FBI chief J. Edgar Hoover who used his knowledge as a hold over them.

The Mob probably helped JFK to the White House but any relationship started to fall apart after Bobby Kennedy began to attack organised crime. Frank Sinatra was furious when the President cancelled a visit to his home because he was worried about Frank's alleged Mafia connections.

There were indirect links between the fight game, the Kennedys and the Mob. They sprang from the lively mix of investors, chief executives, lobbyists, failed politicians, bankers and entrepreneurs who gather round every President. They are people the Mob has an interest in and the 'wise guys' need a connection.

So, well educated, well informed and charming they join the inner circles, offering help and advice, money and muscle, whatever works best. Boxing might be used as an introduction. An appearance by a world champion at a favourite charity event, for example, can be arranged. It's the kind of thing that makes the world go round and Runyon was a keen observer.

A side effect of Sonny's high profile when he was world champion was the extra attention J. Edgar Hoover gave him. He may have been hoping that through Sonny he could link Martin Luther King to the Mafia. A desperate thought, but he was a desperate man.

After Sonny beat Patterson for the second time a PR man was brought in to work with him to soften his image and prepare him for role in society. Sonny had a natural affinity with children and he visited a home for abandoned and orphaned children, offering his time freely, taking a genuine interest and giving the kids someone to look up to. He made a good impression on the kids and staff alike. Beneath the intimidating glare that was designed to keep strangers at a distance there was a very different character. According to the respected author and Civil Rights champion James Baldwin, Sonny was "very complicated, very dedicated, very spiritual".

Before the first Patterson fight Baldwin interviewed Sonny and wrote an essay. He wanted Floyd Patterson to win, thinking it would be better for Civil Rights, but said he found a different Liston to the one he was expecting.

He found someone with aspirations of community service and social leadership. After he won the championship Sonny had said he wanted to use the position in a positive way but the journalistic hype against him was strong and the message was lost.

Baldwin said Sonny reminded him of "Big

Men" he had known who had a reputation of being tough but "weren't hard at all."

He said they used the reputation as a shield. The author even described Sonny as a "Teddy Bear". But of course, he didn't meet him in the ring.

There are many stories of Sonny's personal generosity. A sparring partner who was looking at some jewellery for his girlfriend but couldn't afford to buy was suddenly presented with two full trays, bought for him by this 'mean hard man'.

A driver taking Sonny through heavy traffic was told to stop as he noticed a woman sitting on the kerb, trying to sell odds and ends. The champion sprinted through the cars and dropped a roll of notes into her box. Race didn't come into it the driver said later. She was white.

"I feel the colour of my people's money is the same as anyone else's. They should get the same seats"

Sonny Liston

This was the way Sonny laid it out before his first fight with Ali.

He was the one calling the shots on Civil Rights and against segregation in theatres showing the fight. Not Muhammad Ali, future spokesman for the Nation of Islam.

The result of Sonny speaking out was that venues in New Orleans couldn't screen the fight. Jack Nilon who was Sonny's manager at the time told them he would pull the plug if they didn't change their policy on segregated seating.

They said they couldn't, or wouldn't, so the fight wasn't shown in New Orleans, Montgomery in Alabama, Jackson in Missouri and Waco, Texas. Other cities including Atlanta, Jacksonville and Knoxville accepted Sonny's terms and showed it.

Sonny was reluctant to speak in public about Civil Rights and preferred to keep his feelings to himself. His early beginnings and treatment as a young adult left him suspicious and wary. Sonny was always hassled by the police and sometimes it was understandable – from a cop's point of view. After an argument one finished up in a trash can.

But very often Sonny was hassled because he was big, black, successful – and talked back. Not always though, he sometimes decided the best way to get along was to keep his thoughts to himself.

He did begin to think about a new role as a World Champion. Attacking the media cliché about Sonny in an essay the first thing James Baldwin said was "Sonny Liston is not stupid." He described how

Sonny wanted to be seen as a social leader. Speaking out and forcing cities in the south to do things his way was a big step.

In the past Sonny had tried to avoid civil rights when questioned. Asked why he didn't march with protesters in Alabama he joked, "Because I ain't got no dog-proof ass." This was a reference to the way police in Alabama had set dogs on marchers.

These were violent times. Martin Luther King and two Kennedy brothers were killed. Malcolm X, who spent time convincing Ali he should join the Muslims, was also killed – by his former colleagues in the Nation of Islam after he split from them.

Sonny was very suspicious of the Muslims. He didn't like their attitude to women and he didn't agree with the lifestyle. After a chat with some hippies in LA around that time he said, "These cats have got it right, they don't worry about a damn thing."

Even so, maybe he thought the Muslim threats were serious. He had good reason to believe so, more important people than him had been killed.

All we know for certain is that he lived to fight another day and went on winning, 15 of his last 16 fights. Sonny was a winner and in his first fight with Ali - he won one for Civil Rights.

When Sonny Was In The Picture with Picasso

Before the first Ali fight Sonny's status was recognised in a Christmas cover for the magazine Esquire. The idea came from George Lois, a New York advertising man, an art director with an eye for a great shot.

The cover featured a close up of the intimidating Liston stare, glaring out from the cover. But to counterpoint that impression Sonny was wearing . . . a jaunty Santa hat.

At the time Sonny was freely referred to as the bad guy. That was partly due his frightening physical presence and his brutal toppling of the popular Floyd Patterson from the heavyweight throne. But mainly his reputation as a fighter owned by the Mob - and a man with a criminal record.

The reaction was summed up by a journalist at the time, 'No one wanted to see this cat come down their chimney'. In the atmosphere of racial tension and riots in the sixties, the cover created a sensation.

Esquire lost heavily as advertisers pulled out. But an arts critic latched onto the fear and destructive power of Liston. He described the shot as 'one of the greatest social statements since Picasso's Guernica'. He was referring to Picasso's painting of the savage bombing of Guernica in the Spanish Civil War when hundreds of civilians including women and children were massacred.

The emotions of the day were such that this did not seem an overstatement. Racial fear was in the air, police beatings were on the streets and President Kennedy called out the National Guard. The pretences of Christmas goodwill and racial equality were exposed. A troubled culture split wide open.

Sonny's life and career may have mirrored the worst of times. But his rise to world champion from nowhere gave a glimpse of the possibilities too.

Sonny's physical presence would quiet a room. He said very little amongst strangers but the most intimidating thing about him was the fixed, unsmiling stare that won him the nickname Old Stoneface. This was the man Ali decided to challenge, verbally, in a Las Vegas casino before the first fight.

Sonny liked to gamble. He was throwing dice, and losing, when Ali started taunting him. "Look at that big ugly bear," he said. "He can't even throw dice properly." Ali even knocked the dice out of his hand.

Most of all, Sonny was surprised. Nobody behaved like that around him. It fixed his opinion of Ali, he thought he was crazy. He got up, grabbed Ali by the throat and pushed him against a wall. "If you don't get out of here in 10 seconds I'm going to whip you right here." Ali left, at speed.

Afterwards he admitted Liston had scared him. He remembered all the times he'd been told about the fights Sonny had outside the ring. Looking at him in that moment he knew they were true. Later that night on another floor Liston saw Ali again. He went up to him and slapped him across the face, almost like a child. It was the ultimate put-down, Ali had nothing to say.

Naturally the story got around and a journalist asked Sonny why he had done it. "He was running his mouth. "

"Was it a hard slap?" In reply, Sonny just shrugged, "I didn't have no gauge." For him the incident was over.

As the world knows two contests in the ring had a different ending. Maybe the meeting in the casino confirmed Sonny's misjudgement that this was a lightweight fighter who could be easily swatted away. He didn't train very hard and paid for it.

It's possible a similar error of judgement cost him his life. One of the theories about his death is that he had begun to threaten his old Mob bosses who he claimed owned him money. Maybe the Kennedy brothers made a similar mistake, thinking that from the White House, they could handle the Mob.

Sonny and the Kennedys belonged to the same era. If JFK had lived to win a second term and been succeeded by Bobby the world might be a different place. Given a shot Sonny might have regained the

World Championship, certainly he had a chance against Jimmy Ellis and a developing Joe Frazier.

But enough of the maybes. Let's end by remembering what some people said about Sonny the fighter. The esteemed boxing historian Hank Kaplan said Sonny Liston was amongst the top heavyweight champions of all time. "He had the best jab ever." The shot was painfully remembered by many fighters. Chuck Wepner told how his body was in shock for two days after fighting him and "From round five I was target practice".

Finally Sonny himself when he was asked what was the biggest mistake his opponents made.

"Getting in the ring with me".

Printed in Great Britain
by Amazon

27520293R00051